Fantastical Designs

Coloring Book #4

18 Fun Designs + See How Colors Play Together + Creative Ideas

MEET THE ARTIST:
Paula Nadelstern

Photo by Marianne Barcellona

Paula likes kaleidoscopes. She really, really likes kaleidoscopes. A kaleidoscope is a tube that contains mirrors and things like beads or glass. When you look through a kaleidoscope, you see a beautiful pattern.

Kaleidoscopes are full of surprise and magic, because each time a kaleidoscope moves or turns, the image is unique—which means, just like you, it is the only one of its kind. Turn the kaleidoscope again, and the image is gone. It won't be repeated again.

Paula designs fabric and makes quilts that look like what you see when you look through a kaleidoscope. She also collects kaleidoscopes—she has over 100 of them! Some of her ideas come from her kaleidoscope collection.

The patterns in this coloring book are some of Paula's original fabric designs. She likes designs that use as many colors as possible and have a lot of details. Her fantastical designs give your imagination a lot of room to play—you can use so many colors in them.

Paula lives in New York City, on the same street where she grew up.

Paula would like to thank the artists at Benartex, the company that makes her fabrics. They help turn Paula's designs into fabric that quilters and sewists love to use. She gives special thanks to Kay Saniga, Ruth Beck, David Lochner, Susan Neill, and Susan Kemler.

Do You Know How Fabric Is Designed?

All the fabric that you see around you—from your clothes to your bedspread—is designed by fabric designers. Fabric designers are artists, and fabric is like big blank pieces of paper to them. Depending on how the fabric will be used, they decide what it will look like. It might have a lot of bright colors and geometric shapes such as circles and triangles. Or it might have colors from nature and feature flowers.

Artists (including fabric designers) often use color wheels to find good color combinations to use. Be sure to look inside the back cover for a color wheel that you can use to see how colors play together.

FunStitch STUDIO

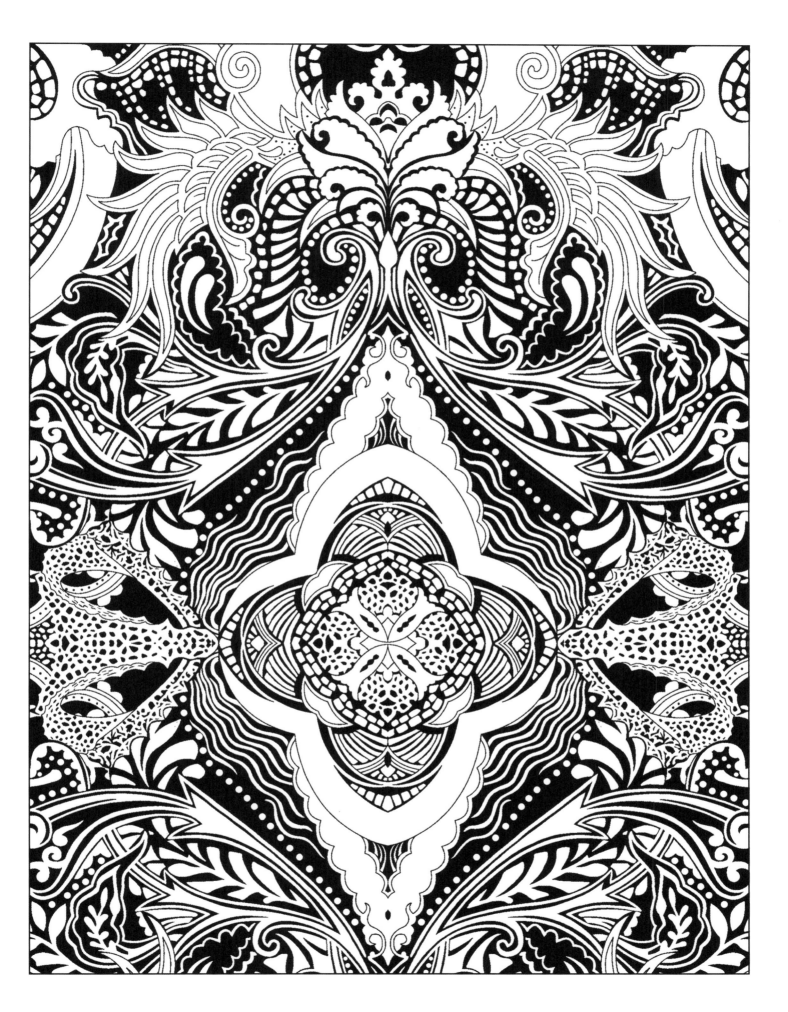

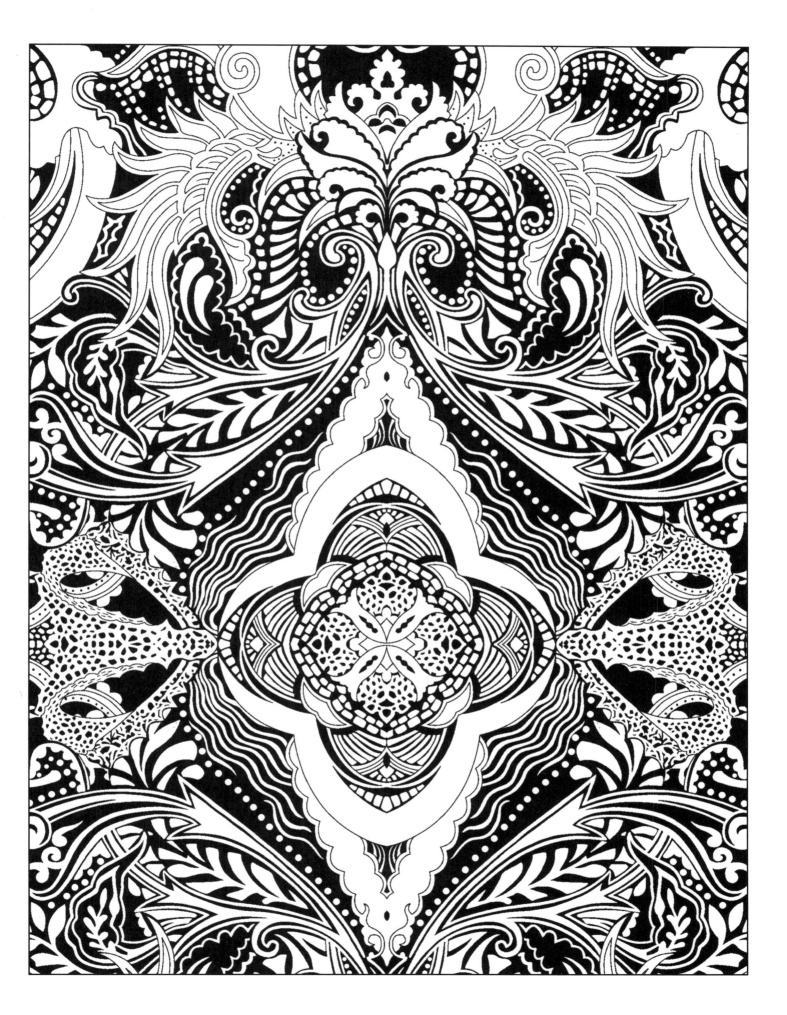